HOW TO TALK TO ANYONE

Master Small Talk, Avoid Awkwardness, Hold Attention and Improve Your Social Skills

---

RICHARD KING

Contents

Introduction

Perhaps you have been in the uncomfortable position where you wanted to have a conversation with a stranger; however, you were at a loss for words? Have you ever wished you could learn to start conversations easily? These skills are not so difficult to learn. Learning to make small talk is the same as learning any other skill. The most important thing when learning any new skill is to practice as much as possible. In order to learn to talk with a stranger, learn a few techniques of conversational skills, then practice, practice, practice until you are comfortable making small talk.

One thing you will want to do before initiating small talk is to make eye contact first. The reason for this is that you do not want to startle your conversation partner. In addition, you want to make sure that they will hear what you say. The best way to ensure that they know you will speak to them is to take a moment of eye contact before saying anything.

The next step in opening a conversation is to comment on your environment. A question about something that both you and your conversation partner can see or experience will make the small talk more comfortable. For example, "I have heard good things about the book you are reading. How do you like it? Avoid subjects you are not both experiencing. For example, a comment like "What do you think about the new governor?" is not something you can both see or experience. A comment like that will give the impression that you are forcing a conversation.

When learning conversational skills, listen carefully to what the person says and be prepared for an appropriate response. Don't make the mistake of asking questions that could be answered with just a yes or no since this will cause the conversation to come to an abrupt end halt.

Try not to ask many questions after each other; this may give the impression that you are conducting an interrogation. On the other hand, don't talk only about yourself; this may give you a self-centered image. Try to talk more about the other person than about yourself. Don't forget in the early stages learning how to talk to anyone may be awkward. However, the more often you do it, the simpler it will be. This book discusses how you can talk to anyone and confidently make small talk.

How To Talk To People

Unfortunately, many people have forgotten or do not know how to talk to people in today's fast-paced world. We have become so focused on ourselves that we think those around us are here for our purposes: we are owed something. This sort of thinking is always more 'demanding' than it is asking and is more about 'me' than it is 'you.' This kind of thinking comes out in the way we talk to people, and we can always see it when such people talk to us.

What's interesting is that we know how it feels to have someone talk to us in ways that disregard our input or minimize our equality, yet many of us do the very same thing to others that we don't like them doing to us.

There are various reasons we do this, but the leading reason is that we have learned and made a habit of doing so. Since it's something we have learned, it becomes possible to change it by learning new ways of talking to people.

Here are some things you can do to make your next conversation with someone a better one:

Keep it simple.

Keeping it simple is a key to practically every relationship or friendship we enter or are involved with.

Not many of us enjoy talking with anyone we perceive as being complicated. They're generally easy to identify because all they do is talk, and usually exclusively about themselves. Take the example of those experiences and apply them to how you talk to people.

Keep it simple, concise, and as direct and to the point as possible. When you explain something to someone else, break it down into small little pieces that are easy to understand and comprehend.

Many people like to show off their intelligence by using those big words they put into their college thesis. This might be okay if the person you are talking to is your college professor. However, most people you will talk to will not be of that intelligence level, so why talk to them like they are? It only shows your lack of consideration for them and that you are showing off when you do.

Most people like communicating with those who speak in a simple and clean language they can understand.

However, to use foul or street language to talk to your employer, teacher, parents, and many others demonstrates your lack of intelligence and command of language usage, rather than how cool you are.

Let the other lead.

Everyone wants to be a Rock Star! And we are at certain times, but we can't be all the time. So there are times when we have to let go and sing back-up and let the other take the front stage and lead the conversation's direction.

Knowing when to do this will dramatically help you talk to people more effectively.

Letting the other lead talking shows that you don't have to control the conversation to know you are a part of it. People appreciate this kind of attitude in the people they are talking to.

Show understanding.

We all want to be understood, and there is perhaps nothing worse than talking to someone who nods in acknowledgment of what we are saying, but when asked what they think, look at us with vacant eyes as if asking, "what did you say?"

This is, in fact, very rude and a good way to end a conversation on bad terms. Instead, when someone is speaking to you, be interactive with them and show sincere interest. You do this by asking questions about what they are talking about and giving your input at the appropriate times.

This is how to talk to people in a respectful, simple manner in which they can understand. It facilitates conversation as the other person is better able to respond and feel comfortable doing so.

How to Talk to Important People

Often, if we struggle in a conversation, it is because we are nervous or self-conscious. That can become even more of a problem when talking with those we consider important. However, you can learn how to talk to important people and feel comfortable doing it.

That is a good thing because sometimes we all have to talk to important people! **Here are a few tips to help you do just that:**

Consider your approach.

This is probably the most important aspect of talking to important people because it makes you think about every aspect of how you communicate.

Really, in communication, the only thing you have to fear is the other person not understanding your point or being offended by what you say or how you say it. You can rectify all these errors by getting your approach correct, so in that respect, talking with someone important is just like talking to anyone else.

Show respect.

You should show respect to anyone you communicate with, but that matter can get a little more complex when speaking to important people. It depends on what makes them important.

For instance, if you are talking to top politicians, royalty, high court judges, etc., an additional aspect of showing them respect is using their proper title to address them. There may also be other etiquettes to follow.

However, if this is not the case, and you are talking to someone important because they are your boss, your future parents-in-law, a potential client, etc., then ordinary everyday respect will suffice. That is the key to this communication, and our remaining points unpick that 'respect' idea is a little more.

Listen to the other person.

Everyone, no matter who they are, is important enough to be listened to. You should actively listen so that you pick up not only on the subject matter of what they say but also so that you can read between the lines and decipher their feelings on it.

Let the other person speak.

Listening well also means allowing the other person to speak freely. That will help them to feel respected and gain a favorable impression of you. That is probably what you want to happen.

Have a stack of safe topics.

There may be certain topics off-limits when talking to a particularly important person; those topics depend on how that person is important to you.

If you know what topics would be improper to speak off, such as company politics with your boss or White house secrets to the President, steer clear of them. It's not smart or funny to raise these topics in conversation and may cause embarrassment to the other person and then ultimately to you.

Instead, think up a list of easy topics of conversation they will probably have an opinion about, which they will not feel judged by sharing with you. That should help the conversation to flow nicely, whoever you are talking with.

Use appropriate body language.

Your body language says a lot about what you are thinking and feeling. That can be a major aspect of talking to important people. Due to their status, they will probably be expecting respect from you, so make sure your body language shows that as well as your words.

Be careful not to invade the personal space of the person you are talking to. Also, don't touch them unless you know them very well and know that such a touch will be welcome. An unwelcome touch can feel very threatening and can ruin a conversation.

If you follow these few simple rules, you will soon feel at ease talking to important people as it is much the same as talking with anyone else. Everyone deserves your respect in a conversation, and now you know how to show it.

How to Talk to Strangers

Unless you are a particularly self-confident person, knowing how to talk to strangers is something that is likely to make you feel a bit nervous, but this is a problem that can be overcome with a little effort.

1. First of all, it's a case of 'practice makes perfect.' The more that you talk to strangers, the easier it will become. You can start off in a small way. For example, if you are waiting at the bus stop, pluck up the courage and make an innocuous remark about the weather, or the unreliability of the bus service, to the person standing next to you. It is very unlikely that you will meet with a rebuff.

Taxi drivers and hairdressers are usually notorious for chatting to their customers, so instead of ignoring or rebuffing them, use it as another practice session. Then, keep on practicing; pass a friendly comment to the super-market cashier, the clerk at the bank, and the receptionist at the doctor's surgery, rather than just stating your busi-ness. By doing this, your confidence will increase in leaps and bounds, and you will find it easier each time that you do it.

2. At parties, conferences, or other social events, if you cannot immediately see anyone you know, instead of hiding in a corner, try to make new acquaintances.

Look out for someone else who is standing on their own, and if they look approachable, go over and start a conversation. If you don't feel that you can walk up to them just like that, take over a tray of nibbles as an excuse, introduce yourself, and then you can strike up a chat.

Always begin with small talks, such as, 'Isn't this a lovely room?' or 'It's a good turn-out, isn't it?' This will not make the other person feel threatened and will give them an opening for something to say back to you.

. . .

3. In order to sustain the conversation, you will need to keep a flow of questions and answers going, particularly if the other person is shy too. Don't get too personal at first, but you can discuss films and TV programs, sporting events, music, and so on.

Later on, if things go well, you can ask about their job, family, etc. But, again, listen attentively to what the other person has to say, and don't interrupt or talk over them. Instead, smile, nod, and make eye contact with them to show that you are interested in what they have to say.

4. If you find that you have nothing in common with the other person, they are unbearably boring, or have nothing much to say for themselves, find a polite excuse to terminate the conversation. This can be something along the lines of, 'Oh, I'm sorry, do excuse me, but I've just spotted my friend Sarah over there, and I have to talk to her. It's been lovely chatting with you.' That way, you won't hurt their feelings.

5. It can be even more difficult if you find yourself having to chat with a whole group of strangers, for example, during a break at a conference

If you feel nervous, try to stand on the outskirts of the group at first and listen to what the others have to say until you feel confident enough to join in with the conversation.

In this situation, the obvious topic of conversation will be the content and presentation of the conference itself, so if you have been paying attention, you are just as well equipped to talk about this as any of the other delegates. So think about what you are going to say, rather than just blurting something out, and that way, you are less likely to risk making a fool of yourself.

Learning how to talk with strangers is intimidating, but your self-confidence will grow with practice, and you will gradually find that it is easier and easier to do. Remembering that the other person is probably just as shy and nervous as you can also be a big help.

How to Talk to Quiet People

Sometimes it can be difficult to work out how to talk to quiet people. That makes us feel awkward when we don't know what to say to break the ice and start the conversation, but often you will find that once you have made that first move and opened up the conversation, even with a quiet person, that gets them warmed up and the conversation will flow from that point.

Here's how to get started on talking with quiet people:

Get your approach right.

Often, people are shy because they feel intimidated or feel what they say will not be well received and may even be scorned or laughed at. That's why it is really important to approach shy people in a friendly manner, without confrontation, so that they feel comfortable talking to you.

Ask questions.

It is unlikely that a quiet person will get the conversation started, so you're probably going to have to do that. Don't worry about that, though. You can easily get the conversation going with a question.

You should ask an open question that cannot easily be answered with a simple 'yes' or 'no' that will kill the conversation before it has even started. But don't feel that the question has to be a smart or intelligent one either. That can be a bad thing.

Good questions to open conversations are very simple ones that ask for the other person's opinion, and it is a question that cannot be answered wrongly. So, ask what they did for Christmas, or where they are thinking of going on vacation this year, or something like that. Then, they won't feel judged and will be more likely to speak to you and give you avenues to develop the conversation.

Show patience.

Quiet people may take a little while to formulate their responses or may answer in short sentences, to begin with. Don't get impatient with that and give them up as a boring person that is not worth talking to.

Listen actively.

Listen actively, and you will find little snippets of the answer, which you can pick up on and use to develop the conversation on terms that the quiet person will probably find easier to respond to, as they provided the information.

Find good topics.

If you show patience and actively listen to the quiet person, you should soon find topics that they find more engaging and easier to talk about. Those are ones on which they are comfortable and have an opinion.

Try to steer the conversation more towards these topics, and they should provide possibilities for lots of supplementary questions with which you can keep the conversation flowing.

Build their trust in you.

Often, quiet people are that way because they feel they cannot trust others if they open up to them. Perhaps they feel you will laugh at their opinion or confront them about it.

It's your responsibility in the conversation to prove that you are trustworthy, and they can talk to you without being judged or without some other negative reaction from you. That will make them more willing to talk to you.

Suggest an activity.

If you find that you and the quiet person have a mutual interest, suggest that you do that activity together. It can be anything, e.g., ice skating, walking, cinema, etc.

This will **have several advantages:**

- You will have more things to talk about related to the activity.
- You will probably find it easier to chat during the activity, as part of their mind will be on the activity itself and not on how tense they feel about conversing, so the talk should flow more naturally.

Give some positive reinforcement.

We all need some positive reinforcement from time to time. That can be especially so for quiet people who might lack the confidence to talk much. Let them know that you enjoyed talking with them and perhaps make time to chat again. That will give a quiet person a real boost.

So, these few tips for how to talk to quiet people will help you talk to anyone, but they will particularly help you coax a quiet person out of their shell and converse with you more comfortably.

How to Talk with Shy People

Taking with shy people requires a unique approach. First, you need to help them trust you and get comfortable with having a meaningful conversation. **Here are some tips to get you started:**

Be positive.

It's hard to stay shy around a positive person. The energy of a positive person is very contagious. Once the shy person catches it, it will naturally make them feel more comfortable and open up in social interaction.

Fortunately, even if you're not in a positive mood, you can make yourself positive. The methods to do this include remembering positive experiences, moving/jumping around, and smiling.

Be curious.

Shy people have a hard time opening up because they think nobody is interested in them and what they have to say. Show them this is not the case when interacting with you, and they'll be a lot more talkative.

Start with asking the shy person open-ended questions. Then, continue listening to what they have to say and manifesting a genuine interest in them.

Be nice.

Shy people are afraid that others will judge them and make fun of them. This is why they hesitate to share their thoughts and emotions. So, when the shy person does open up, prove to them that you do not judge them.

You do so by not making fun of their ideas, avoiding contradicting them, looking for the value in what they have to say, finding commonalities between the two of you, and giving them honest compliments.

Have patience.

Shy people do open up and enjoy social interactions, but they need more time than the average person. This is why it's important to have patience with them and keep making conversation until you reach that point.

Eventually, they open up and are usually very grateful that you've managed to get them out of their shell. Shy people tend to have few friends, but those they do have, often value life.

How to Talk to Successful People

Most individuals are intimidated by successful people, and they don't know how to talk to them, which is why they often avoid them, thus missing great opportunities in their life.

Here are some of the ways on how to talk to successful people successfully and clear this issue once and for all:

The first thing that's really crucial for you to understand is that successful people are not very different from regular people. They have a high proficiency in a certain area, which they've managed to capitalize on very well.

So, for the most part, talking to successful people is the same as talking to regular people. Try not to think of a successful person differently than you would think of your grandma or your next-door neighbor. And talk to them from this mindset.

This is a great mindset to have, above all because it helps you remain calm and composed around thriving indivi-duals, which means you will be able to be as fluent and logical when you converse with them as with any other person.

It's also great because it shows you're not intimidated by success, and you're comfortable with it. Most successful persons love this. Plus, believe it or not, they usually don't want others to put them on a pedestal, and they feel repelled by individuals who kiss their asses or tremble in front of them.

There are two things to take into account, especially when talking to successful people. The first is to show appreciation for their success. Achievement is an achievement, and it's a good idea to respect it.

Don't be afraid to tell a successful person that you appreciate their work or their achievements, if that is true. Even if they've heard it a million times, they'll still enjoy it if it's genuine.

But don't say this in a weak, needy way. Instead, remain calm and have poise when doing this. The appreciation shown with dignity and confidence has much more value than appreciation shown with visible nervousness.

The other thing is not to waste successful people's time. These individuals tend to be particularly busy, and although they may be willing to give you some of their time, it's important not to squander it.

Talk about relevant topics for them, try to add value to the discussion, avoid clichés and stay away from pointless small talk. Keep everything straight and to the point. That's how most persons with serious achievements like it.

One last thing to keep in mind is that, like anything else, learning how to talk to successful people is something you achieve through practice.

So, go out there, participate at various social events, meet successful individuals, introduce yourself to them and talk to them, trying to apply the advice shared in this book.

The more you'll practice, the better you'll become, and the easier it will be to talk to successful people. Of course, until one day, it will be a walk in a park. But, success is much easier to obtain when you know how to talk to people and have good things to talk about.

2

How To Talk With Confidence

Having confidence in yourself can make a world of difference in relating to the outside world. If you fear what is out there, you won`t accomplish much toward your reason for being here. Each of us has a purpose, whatever that purpose might be. And we all have to discover it for ourselves. But in that discovery, you will find your confidence growing, and you will uncover how to talk with confidence.

We all have varying degrees of confidence, and it can change from challenge to challenge. For example, many people don't have the confidence to talk with people. They are easy to identify because they have that look of "I want to say something, but I'm scared" on their faces.

These people listen attentively and are interested in the discussion but may feel that their contribution will get laughed at. If you are one of those people who doesn't have confidence when talking to others, what follows is for you.

· · ·

Here are some pointers on how to talk with confidence:

Slow down.

Many people who lack confidence in talking with others will sometimes talk so fast when allowed to talk that those who are listening quickly get lost in what is being said.

If you are talking too fast for people to understand you, they will turn you off, and this will further damage your confidence in talking with others. To preserve what confidence you have, relax and talk at a moderate talking speed.

Practice speaking with confidence.

Confidence is something we build with practice and experience. There is not one baseball pitcher ever born with the confidence of striking batters out. The pitcher had to practice and improve his skill, and in that comes the confidence he needs to strike a skilled batter out.

Every chance you get, practice speaking with confidence. Talk to yourself in your mirror as if your reflection was another person.

Increase your vocabulary.

Having a good verbal repertoire will help you talk with confidence because you are more verbally flexible. And believe it or not, people who can clearly understand what's being said and then can clearly express themselves are people that most people find interesting to be in a conversation with.

Sounds simple? It is! You can quickly and easily increase your vocabulary by committing to learning one new word a week.

Look into their eyes.

If you lack confidence in talking to anyone, don't show it. One of the best ways you can do this is by looking into the other person's eyes when you are talking, even if you don't feel confident inside.

First and foremost, looking into the eyes of the person you are talking to says you are sincere and confident. When someone doesn't look you in the eye while talking with you, it could indicate shame or that they have something to hide.

Don't give that impression to anyone.

Watch the red flags.

There are red flags that can send a message to the other person you don't have confidence in.

The questions "You know?" and "Right?" are two examples of red flags of someone who doesn't have confidence and needs to hear the other person's affirmations. Unfortunately, those two are unprofessional in the business world, and in severe cases, very annoying.

These questions can positively encourage listening and agreement but never question this out of a need for approval. If you do, the lack of confidence you are expressing will negatively impact the conversation.

Feel confident.

Let yourself experience the feeling of confidence in those moments that you are feeling confident. Your confidence can be built and reinforced best when you can see it and experience it.

There's a saying somewhere that indicates if you act confident, you will become confident. There is a lot of truth in that.

Many people need confidence, or more of it when talking with other people. Following these points will show you how to talk with confidence.

How to Talk without Arguing

Talking to another person without arguing is not an impossible feat.

Knowing how to talk without arguing is strictly an issue of self-control when it comes down to it.

Look to many of the world's leaders. Without a doubt, world leaders become angry while negotiating with other leaders. Although there are disagreements among them, they talk to each other and control themselves; They do not argue, even though they probably want to.

These leaders have the same human feelings as the rest of us do, but a high level of self-control. This is the key to talking without arguing.

. . .

Here are some tips to help you have self-control and to talk without arguing:

Stay focused on the issues.

Nothing can turn a disagreement into an argument faster than losing focus on the issues. Likewise, digressions, transgressions, accusations, or anything else that detracts from what either of you is saying will result in an argument.

If you, or the person you are talking to, lose focus, immediately bring the discussion back to the original disagreement.

If that doesn't work, then agree to end the conversation before it becomes an argument.

Control your tongue.

Even subtle insults couched in a statement can turn a productive conversation into an argument. And using profanity will only get it in return, thus escalating the discussion into an argument.

You can almost always avoid an argument by watching how you are talking to the other person. Again, use self-control.

When you get too angry, step away.

Here too, it's about self-control, but more importantly, identifying when it's time to change the subject or remove yourself from the conversation. You will know your body signals that indicate arising anger, and when you sense that kind of arousal, you need to remove yourself from the situation.

Remember that you're not always right.

Many conversations turn into arguments because someone has to be right.

Don't think that because you are right about some things, it means you're right about everything. If you know everything, then what is your purpose here amongst us human beings? To lead us? Good leaders make mistakes too.

Stop with the excuses.

A conversation can blast off into an argument when the people involved starting making excuses for themselves.

Some people will talk to you about unacceptable behavior, for example. By making an excuse for it, you have already placed yourself in a defensive position. If the one who is talking to you pushes on that position, it could ignite an argument.

The best thing to do is not make excuses and avoid complicating the conversation.

Don't tell lies or fabricate a story.

There is almost nothing worse in a conversation than to lie or make up stories. Practically every person, even criminals, doesn't like being lied to, and it's a guaranteed argument starter when the lie is discovered.

So, save yourself the grief of a heated argument and be truthful and honest.

Give respect, and you could prevent an argument.

Some people can become disrespectful toward the person they are talking to. For example, it's disrespectful for a man to eye a woman up and down while he's talking to her. This will most certainly make her feel uncomfortable, and that could change a friendly meeting into an argument.

Watch that your body language and words are not sending a disrespectful message.

You can talk to other people on some quite difficult topics without arguing. Still, it does take self-awareness and self-control to keep a constructive conversation from sliding down into an argument.

The above tips can help you learn how to talk without arguing.

How to Talk to People, and Confidently Make Small Talk

Talking to people and confidently making small talk is a big bother among many who are worried about their social skills. It has become a focus of media, and clinical attention as the need for conversational skills for success is growing by the day.

Talking to people is the basis of a successful presentation. People judge you by expressing yourself, and conversation skills play a big part in the workplace and social gatherings. Usually, we talk to people whom we know and with whom we share something in common.

But talking to unknown people effectively for the first time would involve conversation starters that can break the ice. While trying to break the ice, we should not appear too interested or be seen asking too many questions.

Knowing how to talk to people can get you places. You can succeed in your business or job and hit off socially if you have the necessary social skills. You should allow the conversation to be initiated on topics that are common to almost everyone.

Bringing up a boring point of discussion which few are familiar with can lead to a dead end. You might also end up being a bore, and your conversation starters will fail to take off. Topics should not only be interesting, but if you can bring in some humor along, it could be great.

Allowing other people to speak allows you to bide your time and chip in whenever you find something interesting. You could come in and start conversations after picking up from the other person. By this process, you can confidently make small talk and not appear intruding or too questioning.

Bringing in some funny anecdotes can lighten up the surroundings and provide you the confidence to carry on the conversation. If you initiate a topic that lights up people's interests, you will gain the confidence to talk to anyone.

Knowing how to talk to people and confidently can open many opportunities and be an effective contact-building tool.

3

Small Talk Mistakes You Should Never Make

I f you're not good at small talk, your social life is likely stagnating. Unfortunately, many people talk down the importance of this skill, even to the point of talking trash about it. This mindset is a mistake. Small talk is an essential social skill that serves an important function.

The only people who shouldn't worry about it are those who already have the perfect partner, great like-minded friends, a mentor, and savvy business partners. Could you use one of the former people in your life? Small talk is a necessary step to meeting new interesting people. However, if you lack skills in small talk, you'll have a hard time meeting them.

5 Stupid Mistakes to Avoid in Small Talk

Having a negative view of small talk.

Many people dislike small talk because they view it as pointless chit-chat. These people don't understand its fundamental purpose. If they did, they wouldn't consider it pointless.

At this stage, the conversation isn't supposed to be very meaningful or deep. Instead, the purpose is to open contact with a person you don't know yet.

Perhaps a relationship will follow from this initial contact, and one day you'll get to more meaningful topics.

If you view small talk as pointless, you'll try to avoid it; avoiding it will lead to you missing out on many new connections.

Heavy subjects.

It's great that you take the time to ponder complex and pressing issues. However, save those topics for a later date.

During small talk, it's better to discuss more superficial matters and focus on getting to know the other person during small talk. The aim of this conversation isn't to save the world.

Introducing big issues into the conversation will only kill the pleasant mood you're trying to maintain. So save politics and religion for another time.

Living a boring life.

Living a mundane life is the number one enemy of interesting conversation. When your days consist of a boring job followed by TV, you'll have little to talk about.

To have interesting conversations, you'll have to experience interesting things.

Get out of your daily routine regularly and expose yourself to exciting new experiences. Not only will you have more to talk about, but you'll also spice up your life.

You can start doing this as soon as today. Do anything that is out of the ordinary and get into the habit of searching out new experiences.

Not asking questions.

The conversation is a dance that requires a minimum of two people. If you're the only one talking, you're not connecting with the other person. They might not even be listening. This defeats the purpose of small talk.

If you find yourself in a one-sided conversation, you'll need to get the other person involved as soon as possible.

The best way to do this is to ask questions. This way you'll get a chance to learn more about the other person, which is an important part of developing relationships.

Hiding yourself.

The mistake that many reserved people make is - they don't reveal enough about themselves.

This is a big mistake if you truly want to connect with the other person.

Opening up a window into your life will give the other person a possibility to grab onto something.

If you take too long to reveal things about yourself, you risk the relationship not developing any further than friendly conversation.

You don't have to reveal your life story. Just a little personal information will do. This will allow you to connect faster and ultimately move past the small talk stage.

Small talk is much more than a pointless exchange of words. It's the necessary first step to meet new people and develop these connections into relationships.

Don't let the process overwhelm you. It's not as hard as it may seem. When you change your perspective about small talk, from being pointless to an important first stage to building relationships, you'll automatically notice yourself starting to make the right moves.

Practice small talk as you would any other skill, and prepare to see your social life prosper.

Learning How to Make Small Talk with Strangers

Do you find it difficult to make small talk with strangers? Most of us do. Talking with someone we don't know can make many of us feel very anxious, especially if we happen to be shy.

Why is it so hard to make conversation with strangers? When you first talk with a stranger, you don't know very much about them. You don't know what their interests are. You don't know what kind of a person they are. You don't know if you have anything in common. You don't know if you can trust them. The stranger you are talking with might be someone who hates everything you stand for. They might even turn out to be people you should avoid.

Human beings have always had a bit of wariness when meeting someone new. So it's no wonder that we are often filled with suspicion and fear when we talk with someone we don't know. Don't feel bad; it's a kind of built-in safety mechanism that is supposed to prevent us from getting into trouble when we meet someone new.

In some cases, this built-in safety mechanism works too well. Even when we are talking with a new neighbor or a new co-worker, we overcome anxiety. We worry about what they will think of us if we can't make small talk perfectly, yet everything we say seems to be stupid.

What should we talk about when we are making small talk with a stranger? The truth is, it doesn't matter very much what you choose to talk about in the beginning. It only matters how the rest of the conversation develops.

So many people have trouble starting a conversation with a stranger because they are far too worried about what they will say initially. Mentally they try out and reject many possible openings for their talk. In the meantime, an awkward silence ensues. The mind goes blank.

What matters far more than what you say is how you listen and pay attention to the other person. Instead of focusing on your topics, focus on the answers the other person gives you. You need to pay attention to what the other person says in response to you. You need to keep an eye on their facial expressions and their body language. Watch for signs of interest in a particular topic. This will give you clues about which way to steer the conversation.

When you feel awkward talking with a stranger, don't put yourself down for being nervous. Don't criticize yourself mentally for being imperfect at making small talk. Putting yourself down for being imperfect will make your performance get worse. You will get even more tongue-tied and awkward. Instead, permit yourself to be less than perfect when making conversation, and go on from there.

Permit yourself to make mistakes. Treat small talk with strangers as a skill you want to master. That means you need to have plenty of opportunities to make mistakes. That means you are experimenting and learning. Eventually, you will become better at making conversation with new people.

Learning to make small talk with strangers successfully is a skill that can pay off in many ways. If you are good at making conversation with new people, it will help you to become a successful networker in your career.

Starting up conversations with new people you meet will also help you improve and expand your social life. Who knows where your next friendship or romantic relationship is going to come from?

It just might be the stranger you met while you were chatting at the bus stop.

How to Make Small Talk with People

Small talk is often perceived as fake or shallow, but one tends to be self-conscious if one doesn't know how to make small talk with people. That's because conversations, especially with people you don't know well, often start with small talk.

If people don't know how to do it, they can spend their time in social situations, standing on the sidelines, not speaking, and not being spoken to. That is a shame, and just a few simple pointers on making small talk with people can greatly increase your confidence in social situations.

Small talk is no small matter; it's quite a big deal about how useful it is for bonding people socially; it is a great way to get to know people. Being willing and able to use small talk tells the other person you are interested in them.

In order to get anything back from the people you talk to, though, you have to give something of yourself, or otherwise, it just feels to the other person as if they are being interrogated.

Listening to their answers is very important for them to feel valued and continue speaking to you.

It's a good idea to have a very brief introduction to yourself planned out in your head before you go somewhere where you might be called upon to speak to people that you do not know. Having that little piece of information planned out in your head and memorized will help you to feel more comfortable about the prospect of meeting new people, and you will find you relax more, making small talk much easier.

Your introduction need not be long; in fact, it shouldn't be more than a couple of sentences. It is perfectly adequate to say 'Hi, my name is..." then go on to state why you are at the social event simply; perhaps that might be something like 'I've been friends with the hosts for a few years now or 'I'm looking for a painting for my lounge room.' The person you are speaking to will probably reciprocate in the same way, and you will have found your first piece of common ground because you will know why you are both there.

Again, listening to the answer is very important. That enables you to take cues from what they say to further the conversation. What you say does not need to be very smart or very funny; something which shows a little interest in the other person will work very well. What you are trying to do is establish a connection with the other person, and once you have connected, the conversation should flow more freely.

Remember that you should not fire a long list of questions at the person to whom you are speaking. That will unnerve them and bore them. Instead, if you find some common ground from one of their answers, something you have a story about, or some positive comment to make, tell them that rather than asking another question. They will relax and open up more as the conversation becomes more two-sided and reciprocal, and so will you.

You can start your small talk with a comment about where you both are. That gives you some common ground already. You can talk about the venue or the event, the food or the facilities. Make your comments positive if you can, as this puts people in the best frame of mind to reply to you.

If you're going to a specific event, do a little bit of research beforehand so that you will have some things to say. You don't have to be a world authority; in fact, that can be off-putting.

Having something interesting to contribute will help when it comes to small talk, so keep up with the news and current affairs, what's on at the cinema, etc.

You need to have a few things in your memory bank to say that you're less likely to go blank and silent. So, when it comes to doing small talk with people, practice a two-sentence introduction to yourself and have three or a couple of simple questions you could ask, then look around you and listen to people for further inspiration.

How to Make Small Talk That Isn't Boring

If you've ever been stuck on a first date, at a party, or work with absolutely nothing interesting to say, you've surely wondered how to make small talk without sounding like a robot. People talk about the same, safe topics when they meet new people, resulting in repetitive conversations. This does nothing to build relationships, and it's not even a fun way to pass the time! Most people simply tune out of such conversations or give the standard, expected reply.

It's time to kick those old small-talk habits and learn how to tweak your thinking. There's no big secret about how to make the small talk interesting. It's all about you and how you phrase your questions and answers.

Depersonalization.

This is exactly what it sounds like: removing anything personal from the conversation. Sometimes people do this automatically as a defense mechanism. Other times, we don't feel close enough to a person to reveal how we feel about a subject.

There's no need to resort to talking about topics like the weather. Let's use the weather as an example of how to turn a standard, boring small-talk topic into something fun and interesting. When the topic comes up, don't' simply state that you hate winter. Instead, mention how much you're looking forward to spring. Perhaps you're taking a trip, or maybe you just like to watch things bloom and come back to life. This is a great time to mention your garden if you have one. This is how to make small talk more personal without revealing anything too intimate.

Giving orders and flat opinions.

When we're nervous or bored, sometimes we resort to short, curt answers. This can come off as very cold and make us seem like we think our word is the law. Instead of making a short statement such as "That movie was horrible," try and point out something about it that you didn't like. This will show your thought process and open the conversation up for more opinions. By simply adjusting a statement, you've turned a stale, superior-sounding comment into a lively discussion!

Acting like an interrogator.

You are not a cop. Even if you are a cop, it's best not to act like one while learning how to make small talk. This is another easy trap to fall into asking rapid-fire questions without taking the time to listen or comment on the other person's answers. This can also make you seem as though you feel superior. On a date, it can make the other person very uncomfortable, almost as if you're interviewing them instead of getting to know them. Either way, it's not an easy, fun conversation. This is easy to fix. Simply ask a question, listen, and comment on the answer. Not only will you feel more engaged, but the person you're talking to will feel like they're talking and not just answering.

It's easier than it seems to make these small changes. If you keep a few simple guidelines in your head when on first dates and at parties, you won't be thinking about how to make small talk pretty soon. You'll just be talking!

4

Upgrading Your Small Talk Skills

Do You Need to Upgrade Your Small Talk Skills?

Billions of people are doing it every single day. You could say it makes the world go round. Some of the people who are doing it are very young. Some are very old.

And billions of hours are spent on it every single day.

What is this activity that is so common that nearly everyone is doing it every single day? It's taking part in the conversation! Making small talk! Conversing. Yakking. Making chit-chat. Chatting!

This type of conversation isn't very deep, and it's not about anything important. You could say that on the surface, most conversations between two people are often very trivial. Because these conversations seem to be so trivial, you might think that they are not important, but they play a big part in getting to know other people and how they get to know us in return.

You can have a chat with someone you've known for years. Or with someone you just met in a lineup at the bank. You might want to share the latest gossip or talk about sports. Your conversation partner might ask you how you like the weather or what you do for a living.

This kind of idle conversation might last five minutes, or it might last half an hour. In many cases, small talk conversation doesn't lead anywhere. It just disappears without leaving much of a trace.

Are all those billions of hours that people spend every day making conversation a waste of time? Not necessarily.

Even though a small talk conversation can be a big time-waster, it also helps the time go by. It helps people get to know each other better. Small talk can be a lot of fun and extremely enjoyable.

And even though most small talk conversations might not be about anything important, a few may lead you to form deeper friendships with some of the people you chat with. Or these conversations might lead to new job opportunities.

Small talk has a purpose. The purpose of small talk is that it helps you to get to know other people in a fairly safe and predictable way.

And having good talk skills is important. A lack of conversation skills can lead to problems in creating new relationships. Poor conversation skills can even hold you back in your career.

The purpose of small talk is to let other people know just a little bit about you, while at the same time you get to learn a little bit about them.

During the course of making introductory small talk, you may find that you have some interests in common. Or you may discover that you don't have much to talk about!

The next time you encounter someone that you've already chatted with before, you both will know just a bit more about each other. The more you talk, the more you may find that you have in common.

Not everyone is good at making conversation with people they don't know very well. Some people find making small talk very difficult, even unbearable.

Very shy people and people who have poor self-esteem often have difficulty starting these conversations and keeping them going.

Sometimes very smart people are the ones that have the most difficulty in making idle conversations with others.

People who aren't good at the small talk will find that they don't make nearly as many friends as people who make small talk easily. In addition, a lack of conversation skills can make you look socially awkward.

People who are not good at making conversation can end up feeling very lonely.

If you have problems making small talk and other forms of conversation, what should you do?

First, you must ask yourself whether improving your conversation skills is something you want to do. Then, ask yourself why improving your conversational skills could be important to you.

Would your life be better if you could make conversation easily with other people?

If the answer is yes, the good news is that you really can improve your conversational skills. Of course, it will take practice and commitment to make your conversations better, but it can open up a whole new world of social opportunities for you when your conversation skills improve.

Great Small Talk Questions to Get People Talking

If you are not a 'people person or a good conversationalist, you may find it quite difficult to start the ball rolling and make small talk whenever you are in the company of a room full of strangers. If you do not get over your fears, your inability to make small talk will prove to be a disadvantage and will inhibit you from widening your social circle. Thus, you need to exert some effort into developing your 'small talk skills.'

One aspect of being a good conversationalist is knowing which small talk questions can break the ice and make others respond to engaging in a friendly conversation with you. **Take a look at these small talk questions that you can use to get the conversation going the next time that you make small talk:**

Work-related questions.

"What do you do?" is a sure-fire conversation starter if you do not want to exhaust mundane topics like traffic or the weather. Someone's profession is personal enough to get them talking but not too intrusive, especially if you speak with a total stranger you have just met in a social function. Small talk questions which are work-related will keep the ball rolling.

While you are engaging in small talk, it also helps to listen to how they answer the questions. By listening intently and looking the person in the eye while engaging in small talk, you can gather clues about the aspect of their work that they are most passionate about and take your cue from there.

Questions about their interests.

Finding something that you have in common is one of the keys for a good conversation to take off. When you are engaged in small talk, ask about their interests.

For example, you can ask about the latest movie that they've seen, the type of music that they listen to, or a book that they may have read. This is where you can put to good use your knowledge about a wide range of topics. A lot of people feel comfortable with others who share a common interest.

Family-related questions.

People love to talk about their families. Keeping your tone and your questions casual is the key to making small talk by using family-related questions to keep the exchange of words flowing.

If, for example, you happen to have a glimpse of a family picture, casually ask the person about them and if they have a close-knit family. Do not, however, be overly intrusive since casual acquaintances may not feel comfortable if you delve a bit deeper into their personal life.

Questions about general topics.

Current events, movies, music, fashion, and food are just some general questions you can present when making small talk. If you can make small talk, but you cannot think of anything 'witty' to say, ask questions about general topics that are usually your safest bet. Asking people about their views on current events or world events will express your interest and knowledge about what is happening around you.

Just as it is important to know which questions to ask when making small talk, it is also vital to know how to respond to the subject you are chatting with. These small talk questions should give you enough of an edge to survive any social scene where you need to engage in mundane conversation with other people. By learning how to engage in small talk, you will have additional opportunities to go out and widen your social and even your professional circle.

Great Small Talk Topics for Every Situation

Do you regard finding a small talk topic during conversations to be an arduous chore? You are not alone - many people think that making small talk is a particularly hard thing to do. But there are ways to make finding a small talk topic a much easier task.

Why is making small talk so difficult for some people? Some people find it hard because they may not be confident about their conversational skills - as is the case with foreigners new to using the English language. Or they might not be highly educated, so that they may feel intimidated in the presence of more highly educated people or people in authority. Small talk also gets hard because, even if one person initiates a conversation, the other party may not be inclined to answer or have communication problems of his own.

One party might have religious or political sensibilities that cause him to be defensive or even hostile (which is one reason why it is not recommended for conversation to focus on religious or political topics). Cultural differences may also exist, making one or both parties hesitant to pursue conversation until the common ground can be uncovered.

Here are some tips that should make finding a small talk topic less difficult:

Ask the other party or parties a lot of questions about themselves. Not only is this the polite thing to do, but it also helps move along the conversational ball.

Be sure to listen to the responses to your questions. You would not ask a barrage of questions then not pay attention to the other person's replies. Plus, if you listen closely, the responses to your questions may lead you to ask even more in-depth questions.

Ask questions that are relevant to the other person - such as questions about their background, their family, any friends you have in common, or what he may like to do. This opens up areas in his life that he may have in common with you, posing an opportunity to bond.

Be well-read and well-informed about a host of topics. You have heard it said that it pays to read a lot and it is true - if you know a lot about different topics, you can easily conduct a conversation with people from different backgrounds. It will not be so hard to find a small talk topic then.

Keep the flow of the conversation on a casual keel. You might panic if the conversation takes on a very deep tone, such as when you are talking about politics or business because then it becomes harder to find common ground that you can agree on. Instead, topics should be light, hopefully cheerful to bond better with the other party.

Avoid controversial topics, like asking if the other person is gay. Controversial topics might only put the other person on the defensive. Also, you and the other person might be on opposite sides of the issue.

What are some common topics that you can safely conduct small talk about? For example, **you could initiate small talk about:**

- Sports - almost everyone likes some kind of sport.
- Hobbies
- Weather and climate being experienced
- Your respective spouses and children
- Media - such as television shows, movies, or music that both of you may like.
- Holidays that you think the other person may enjoy (but refrain from talking about how much your holiday cost you - unless the other party brings it up.)
- Your respective hometowns

- General information about the occupation of each person.
- Current trends in art or fashion.
- Gossip about famous people.

Hopefully, all these tips will allow you to have an easier time looking for a small talk topic.

Conversations, Small Talk, and the Secret to Making Friends

Many people often dread small talk. It is seen as the awkward part of all conversations. Small talk comes before a drawn-out conversation or is just a small conversation in itself.

Small talk doesn't require witty stories or much detail. Most people see small talk as something you do a friendly hello or take up time before interesting conversations come along.

In reality, small talk can be interesting, it does not have to be to pass the time, and it does not have to be uncomfortable.

The following tips outline some great pointers for making small talk less of a chore and more fun. In addition, you will find information on what to say, how to ease your nerves, and above all, how to keep small talk from getting out of control.

Set a relaxed tone.

You do not want to give off the feeling that you are uncomfortable with the conversations you have. Instead, you should take control of the conversation, initiate topics, and keep things going.

If you sense the other person is uncomfortable, you should try changing the topic or letting them take over the conversation. The whole idea is that small talk should not feel odd or awkward.

Start out conversations by talking about something obvious.

If you happen to run into an old friend in the store and have a new baby, comment on the baby. If you are meeting someone for the first time and trying to strike up a conversation, look for something about them to talk about.

For example, if they wear a shirt with a cute saying or picture, comment on that. Most people find it easy to talk about themselves, so that is why this is a great place to start.

Ask questions to keep conversations flowing.

Try not to ask the same type of question over and over. For example, do not keep asking why questions. Instead, mix it up a little and use them all: who, what, when, where, why, and how. Of course, keep your conversation questions interesting too.

Try to avoid the mundane questions like, 'Where are you living now?' or 'What have you been up to?'. These worn-out questions can make a person believe you would rather not be having a conversation with them, but you are because it would be rude to walk away.

Use a good topic to base your conversations around.

The main things people talk about during small talk are family, occupation, hobbies, and anything they are passionate about.

You can ask questions and get great feedback. Starting out by asking a question regarding one of these topics will get the other person talking. Likewise, starting out with something they know about will ensure you get them talking.

Remember to keep conversations short.

Nothing is worse than a small talk session dragging out into a full-blown hour-long conversation. But, of course, most people have something else on their schedule when they begin in small talk, so keep that in mind.

If you are interested in what they are saying and wish, you could talk longer, get their email address or phone number and continue the conversation later.

Following these pointers will help you be able to carry on effective and interesting small talk conversations. As a result, you can avoid those strange periods of silence where you never quite know what to say.

You will also be able to make the other person feel good about your conversation. Small talk can be a good time. You just have to know the right way to do it.

Small Talk Tricks

Small talk is a polite conversation about trivial matters that usually do not include much controversy. It involves things that are of no importance, especially between people who do not know each other well.

It revolves around topics like sports, weather, current jobs, the latest gossip, or where an individual lives. It is an unnecessary conversation that tends to fill in a situation that looks awkward. It at times backfires into social discomfort and feelings of loneliness.

On the other hand, small talk helps to build ones' confidence such that you can initiate conversations, develop your social skills and make connections.

Small talk is knowing what to say and what not to say (what to be kept private). When involved in small talk, some things make you or the person you are conversing with uncomfortable.

Some of the things that makes small talk critical include:

- **Financial.** Asking people, you are meeting for the first time about financial issues is quite inappropriate. While it is good to ask someone what they do for a living or positive aspects of their career, it is not appropriate to ask them questions about salary. Some people will find such a question intrusive and inappropriate.
- **Religion.** It is another sensitive and personal question to ask someone you are meeting for the first time. Some may not like it if asked which religion they fall in since they may think you fall on the opposite side; hence may take it as a discrimination question. It is also vital to know

that some people do not belong to any religion; hence such a question may be insulting. Therefore, questions on religion should be avoided during small talk.

- **Politics.** Another area to be avoided is politics. The problem is that you may not know who in the crowd has strong opinions. Avoid political questions unless you are prepared for a heated debate.

- **Sex.** Asking questions of intimate nature or talking about sex during small talk is very untimely. When talking to strangers, stop making sexual innuendos or talking about sex openly. Such questions tend to make other people uncomfortable.

- **Death.** Another worse topic to be avoided during small talk. When in the company of strangers, do not come up with topics that may bring up emotions or potentially upsetting. Some in the group may have lost somebody close to them, and when reminded, they may end up going emotionally about it.

- **Appearance/age.** Dare not ask somebody questions related to age and appearance unless you know the person well. It may look pretty similar to you but a hot topic for someone else. You are talking to a strange woman, and you are asking her if she is pregnant or why she looks so slim or fat. You may not know the reason for the pregnancy, slimness, or fatness, which could leave you and her in an uncomfortable situation.

- **Offensive Jokes.** You hardly know somebody you've just met, and you've started the silly jokes you make with your best friends. Unfortunately, some people don't like jokes. To be specific, avoid racist and sexist jokes as they are offensive and may end your conversation quickly.

- **Personal Gossip.** You may gossip about celebrities during small talk, but avoid gossiping about people you know. Gossiping about other people paints you badly. On the other hand, you never know who may know each other. Stop bad-mouthing!

- **Past relationships.** On the first date, avoid talking about a past relationship. Some people's past may be hurting, while others may not like it when you tell them how your ex used to do good things to you. Talking too much about a past love or making comparisons is a turnoff and a fast way to make you not get a second date.

- **Narrow topics.** Do not talk too much about one-sided topics. It is boring, for example, to go into too many details of a movie when some of the people haven't seen the movie. Instead, be keen and watch signs that show they have lost interest and find a way to end it quickly.

Those are among the many things you should avoid in small talk. They are critical and may quickly end up in conversations. However, do not be scared of small talk. You should learn to overcome the fear of small talk. **Below is a list of the things that can make you handle small talk:**

- **Entertainment and Arts** – Topics on arts and entertainment are good for conversation starters. They may include; books, movies, and TV shows, music, etc.

- **Weather** – as much as it looks mundane, it is a general topic that everyone can discuss. Practice small talk on weather questions, or else you will get yourself in the middle of difficult silence with nothing to start on.
- **News** – reading the news and be updated on current issues is the best way to prepare for the small talk. Be aware of what is trending in your country or city.
- **Family** – You are likely to be asked about your family. Get prepared to answer such questions and to ask them too. This will help you learn about a person within a short period.
- **Celebrity gossip** – It is good to know a little about some popular celebrities should the topic emerge. But unless everyone is talking about the celebrity, avoid being the initiator of such conversations.
- **Hobbies** – If you don't have a hobby, consider having one since people like talking about their hobby and may be interested to know yours too. It will give you something to talk about and know other people with interests similar to you.

Small talk is all about building bridges between you and the other person. What you talk about doesn't necessarily matter, but rather you are just conversing to know more about each other.

5

The Art of Small Talk

Business people, particularly those of you who travel, must be well versed in a variety of areas. You must be efficient packers, good at directions, and adept at lathering ridiculously tiny bars of hotel soap. You must also be skilled at small talk.

Small talk might seem like something that carries little weight, seeming as though it is called small for a reason. However, small talk can open the doorway to all kinds of conversations. It can lead to finding commonalities, discovering similar likes or dislikes, and finding the universal ground of laughter. It can also help you be remembered by those you want to impress. On a business trip, the need to chat may come up more than you think; you don't want to be left winded.

- **Ask people where they are from:** Everyone is from somewhere, and people are often very proud of their roots, yes, even those from Canada. Asking someone where they are from is a great way to start a conversation and find a commonality. It also gives people the chance to tell you a little bit about themselves and allows you a moment to travel the world vicariously.

- **Ask people about their kids:** Sure, this might not apply to everyone; not everyone has children. But, if someone does, asking about their offspring can get both your feet through the conversational door. Parents love to talk about their kids - it allows them to brag about their gene pool subtly. In addition, most people hold their kids as one of their favorite subjects, so feel free to ask away.

- **Ask people about recent events:** Some recent events you probably want to stay away from. Events involving politics, religion, the Iraq war, or the debate over abortion are best kept out of the small talk world. Other events, however, are fair game. Try striking up a conversation by asking people what they thought of the latest Super Bowl or what summer movie they are looking forward to seeing. If you are feeling particularly brave, ask them if they are the father of Anna Nicole's baby.

- **Ask people about television:** Okay, so not everyone watches TV. But, since the invention of TIVO and DVR, there is no excuse not to watch at least an hour or two a week. From 24 to Lost, from Grey's Anatomy to ER, from The Office to, say it with me, American Idol, chances are someone watches what you watch. Discussing a television show, you both find addicting is a great way to form an instant bond...one that won't be interrupted by commercials.

Being well-versed in small talk is not just important for business people; it's a skill that everyone can benefit from. Small talk, after all, is just big talk on a littler scale. However, starting up a small talk conversation often, and doing it well, can help you make friends, form alliances, and learn a little more about the people whose lives cross with yours.

How to Master the Art of Small Talk

Why do many people often talk about the art of small talk? Is there an art to making small talk? Actually, there is.

One person who wanted to propagate the art of making small talk was the late President Franklin Roosevelt.

To see if his listeners were paying attention to him, he would often greet people, saying: I murdered my grand-mother this morning. Most of the time, people did not notice - until he met one alert woman who replied: I am sure she had it coming. Thus, the President proved that most people had neglected the art of small talk.

Making small talk means making pleasant conversation on casual topics. It is different from conversations that pursue deep topics because making small talk means you do not engage in heavy debate about such deep topics.

The point of small talk is to find topics that you and the other party have in common to form deeper ties with the other person. The preferred effect of small talk is to form ties of friendship with the person you are talking to.

Why is the art of small talk deemed important? **It is because small talk can:**

- Create a friendly atmosphere wherein you and the other person can exist.
- Help you make a favorable first impression on the other person.
- Permit two people to learn a lot about one another within a short period of time.
- Help you learn more about a topic that you are interested in.

How can you master the art of small talk then? **There are ten steps to doing so:**

- Before an event where you know you will have to engage in some small talk, try to bone up on various topics you believe will be of interest to all concerned. It helps if you are interested in such topics yourself.
- Avoid controversial topics, too personal or offensive in some way to the other party. (These could include topics such as problems with your health, family, finances, or other personal issues; death; divorce; violent crimes; loss of employment; poor view of the current state of the economy; incidents of famine, pestilence, war, and terrorism; issues that are known to make people react emotionally; religion; politics; and sex.)
- Learn to gauge the receptiveness of other people to the small talk topic you have selected. This means that if the other party gives you subtle vibes that he does not like the issue at hand, you should find a way to excuse yourself politely from

the group and join another group that is more receptive to making small talk.

- Smile and maintain eye contact with the person you are making small talk with. This helps to raise the comfort level for both you and the other party.
- Introduce yourself first, then lead the conversation by asking an open-ended question. Though some people are naturally shy, if you find this hard, let someone ask the first question, then make it a point to join in afterward.
- Make it a point to use the name of the other person in the conversation. This shows the other party that you are paying attention to.
- Listen closely so that you can catch key phrases and words, facts, and opinions vented by other people in the group. This allows you to make intelligent comments yourself.
- Self-disclosure is important because it shows the other people around you that you trust them enough with certain information about you. The trick is knowing how much personal information to disclose.
- Encourage other people to join in by asking for their opinion about the topic.
- Restate information disclosed in the conversation to show you are attentive.

As you can see, the art of small talk can be kept alive if enough people were to follow these guidelines.

The Art of Making Small Talk Sexy

Here are some tips on how to small talk with women. Small talk is an art, and knowing how to small talk will drastically increase your ability to keep a conversation going and make it more enjoyable for the both of you.

We've all been there, some of us quite a few times: You see a woman across the room, you use so much energy psyching yourself up to talk to her (sometimes with the help of some liquid courage) that when you finally do get up to her, you realize that you have nothing to make small talk to her about.

Instead of just standing there in awkward silence, **use the following tips to help make better small talk with women:**

Don't be scared to tease her.

Try to maintain a level of playfulness throughout the entire conversation. If things are going awkwardly, don't be scared to mention the awkwardness and then take out some kind of parlor trick (a high-five, some kind of awful joke, a juggling act) to get rid of the awkward silence. The important thing is to maintain your playfulness.

No matter the specifics of what you two are talking about, chances are she's going to forget them the next day. What she will remember, however, is the feeling that she got during the small talk.

Therefore, if you keep things playful and get her to have a good time in the small talk, that will be just as important as the topics you guys are discussing.

Don't interrogate her.

While I haven't met a woman who doesn't like to talk about herself most of the conversation, you mustn't spend most of the conversation barraging her with questions. Instead of using a rapid-fire approach to learning more about her, use statements after every new topic question. This is how to make small talk that connects with women rather than isolates them.

For example, if you ask her if she has any pets and responds by saying she has three cats, don't immediately ask her what their names are. Instead, comment on the fact that you've "heard cat owners are more independent than dog owners." Now, you can talk about whether or not this study is accurate, which will lead her into talking about herself some more (which she'll love) but without her feeling like you're simply asking her a bunch of questions (which she'll hate).

Tell stories.

Telling stories to a girl you just met is both positive and negative. Positive because she's someone who has never heard any of your stories before, meaning you can tell her anyone you want (and even embellish it a bit, if you're so inclined). Negative because she will use the story you tell to get a better understanding of you. When not talking about her, feel free to tell her a few stories about your life, keeping in mind to make them about the more positive aspects of your life.

Instead of just listening to the specifics of the story you're telling, she'll try to read between the lines to find out just what kind of person you are. For example, if you mention that you had to "wake up early for work" at the beginning of your story, she'll already start thinking about what kind of job you must have that has you wake up so early.

This is something to keep in mind while telling stories: You want to lead her in the right direction by offering subtle clues like that but also keeping in mind that certain asides to the story ("So I woke up at my usual time of 11:30 in the morning") may make you look bad.

Stories are exactly how to small talk in a way that gets a woman engaged. The art of small talk desperately involves the ability to tell a good story.

Non-verbal communication is key.

More important than any of my other tips is the non-verbal communication that goes along with every conversation. You can tell by just looking across a room whether two people are into each other or not, whether or not they're talking about something interesting at all. So make sure you're not fidgeting when you're talking to her and are exuding a presence of calm and confidence. Remember: The actual words that are coming out of your mouth are only worth about half when compared to the tone of voice and how you're saying them.

You can use any of these four tips to make small talk more appealing to women. Many guys are scared, but that is because they don't know how to small talk successfully. Once you figure this out, you'll find flirting and attracting women becomes much easier.

6

5 Powerful Small Talk Tips
That Work Every Time

If you are not much of a talker, you may find that making small talk takes a lot of effort, so why would you even bother? The downside to this thinking is that you are limiting yourself to interacting with the people you already know instead of having the opportunity to broaden your social, professional, and personal relationships.

It does not matter whether you are a good conversationalist or not. You need to be polite, nice, and knowledgeable enough, try to go out of your way to make small talk, and feel the other person comfortable while you two are chatting.

Here are some easy-to-follow tips on how to make small talk so that you can strike up a casual conversation with someone:

Get out of your comfort zone.

If you are the loner type and you'd rather be caught dead than making small talk with a total stranger, you need to bend a little and go out of your way to strike up a casual conversation with someone. Start with a neighbor, a co-worker, a tourist, an elderly person – by conversing with the people you get to see and meet every day, you would get a feel of how it is to casually chat with someone and develop your conversational skills in the process.

Start with something simple.

A friendly "Hello" would go a long way if you want to make small talk. You can follow up this casual greeting by asking the other person about how their day has been so far.

A simple and casual comment - even about something obvious is a signal to the other person that you are willing to make small talk, and you would like to strike up a casual conversation with them.

Listening to what the other person has to say is also part of small talk.

Making small talk is also a two-way street, and you should not be the only one to do all the talking. After making a casual comment about something, try to get the other person to join in the conversation by asking questions. An exchange of words should keep things going.

Listening is also an important part of making small talk. By intently listening, you will give the other person enough confidence to open up to you and give the impression that you are interested in what they have to say.

Be prepared to introduce general topics as a way to start the conversation.

The key to making small talk is to keep the topics varied, casual, and interesting. Neutral topics which are general and not too personal or intrusive include the weather, traffic, current events, work, family, movies, television, funny anecdotes, and a lot more. Finding out that you have something in common with another person is another goal of making small talk, and you may just even be surprised at what you can find out about each other.

Then, when the tables are turned, and the other person is the one who introduces a topic, make an effort to respond by commenting, giving out your opinion, or sharing what you know about the subject.

Do not attempt to make small talk and turn it into a long, drawn-out conversation that could turn out to be awkward, so make your exit gracefully.

One mistake that a lot of people make is trying to extend small talk into an entire conversation. Things tend to take an awkward turn when you run out of things to say. That is why you need to be able to recognize when you can gracefully make your exit, say your goodbyes and tell the other person how nice it is to have a chat with them.

With these tips on making small talk, you can be prepared and breeze your way through the next time you find yourself in a social setting where introducing casual conversation is the polite thing to do.

Making Small Talk Fun - 4 Simple Steps

Small talk has a way of connecting people on some level, and it serves as the starting point of a person or a professional relationship.

Do not worry if you find the thought of making small talk daunting because many people share the same fear. Some cannot bear the thought of rejection, so they would not like to make the first move in starting a casual conversation, while others are intimidated by the thought that they may not know what to talk about!

Like striking up a conversation with a person you like when you are in the dating scene, there are also some 'rules' that you can follow in making small talk.

1. Make a comment on something obvious.

If you are standing in line in a store and it is not moving, casually say to the person next to you, "I wonder what is taking so long?"

Of course, this statement needs to come out pleasantly, in such a way that you will not appear to be whining or complaining.

The weather, traffic, or location are also some of the things that you can comment on.

Since you will only be engaging in small talk, you do not need to come up with a witty or in-depth comment about a particular subject - something simpler or even stating the obvious would be a safer bet.

2. *Try to muster all your self-confidence and use it to make other people feel comfortable.*

When you walk into a room full of strangers, do you keep to yourself, or do you try and mingle? Self-confidence plays an important part in making small talk. Also, the thought of getting another person actually to respond to your comments will take a certain amount of self-confidence on your part.

The key to breaking the ice and engaging in small talk is to make the other person feel as comfortable as possible. Asking questions, listening intently to what they have to say, and finding common points of interest are some of the things you need to do when engaging in casual conversation.

3. *Use humor or your knowledge of a wide array of topics when making small talk.*

The fear of not knowing what to talk about is one thing that prevents some people from making small talk. However, this is the reason why you have to broaden your knowledge of a wide array of topics so that you will have something to contribute to any conversation.

Humor is also a great icebreaker; you can start by sharing a self-deprecating comment when you introduce yourself to get a laugh out of the person you are chatting with. Or, share a brief anecdote about what happened on your way over.

Discussing general subjects like work, sports and hobbies are also good conversation starters.

4. Do not dominate or hog the conversation.

You might have read somewhere that there are two kinds of people. When walking into the room, one would say, "I am here," while another would say, "There you are!." The difference between the two shows that the person who says "I am here" is focused on himself, while the second one focuses more on other people. The same principle can apply when making small talk. Do not let it be all about you. No matter how casual, small talk should involve the other person, so do not hog the conversation. Instead, try to listen and ask about the other person's opinion.

When making small talk, keep these things in mind and know when to make a graceful exit - and in no time at all, you can turn small talk and casual conversation into an art form that you have already mastered.

Proven Methods to Crush it With Small Talk

Knowing how to small talk can help you with women is like saying it good to swim before jumping into the deep end of a pool. It is the difference between moving around effortlessly and flapping around like an uncoordinated drowning chimpanzee. Having the ability to small talk is a major component of attraction.

Failing at small talk makes guys quickly fall into a few categories. First, they either are awkwardly silent. Second, making the girls think they are like "Buffalo Bill" from Silence of the Lambs. Or, perhaps even worse, they try to talk too much in a messy and overly eager fashion making the woman SURE he is desperate and needy.

To bust out these horrible paradigms and learn how to small talk, here are a few very basic but proven methods to crush it with small talk:

- ***No 3rd degree.***

You are not a cop that is trying to get the truth out of a woman. Do not interrogate her. Ask the woman some open-ended questions about herself. Many women like to talk about themselves if she goes into detail, guides the conversation towards what you want to know. If she doesn't want to talk about herself, bring up other things.

- ***Tease.***

Learning to tease is an important part of learning to attract women. One mistake common people make is that they try to put a girl on a pedestal immediately, specifically if she is attractive. Never do this. Do not outright "insult" her, but never be scared to bring a little teasing into the mix.

- ***Body language is a big part of small talk.***

According to many stats, people learn over 90% about a person, not by what they "say" but by what they "do" while saying it. Understanding body language is, therefore, a pretty important concept. There is way too much to go over in this simple and quick guide, but it is important to learn how to project body language that makes you seem confident and self-assured.

- ***Tell stories.***

Let the girl have free reign to talk about herself. If the conversation lags for any reason, make sure that YOU have a good collection of stories to tell.

These should always include stories that make you look good and are about positive things in your life. For example, telling her stories about how you got wasted and barfed all over one girl may be self-effacing and funny to the guys, but it just makes her think "pathetic."

Make these stories well-paced, humorous, and on point. Never drag them out. If you see her looking away from you, something is wrong; wrap it up quickly.

7

4 Secrets To Successful Small Talk

Next to public speaking, making small talk is probably one thing most people dread - or even fear. The thought of coming up with something witty or interesting to say to a stranger, a new acquaintance, your boss, a neighbor - anybody whom you do not normally have a conversation with can prove to be quite a daunting experience. However, you need to make small talk if you want to survive any given social scene.

So take a look at these small talk tips to help get the conversation going:

Be comfortable with who you are.

Self-confidence plays a big role in gathering the courage to go out of your way and engage the new people that you meet in small conversation. If you are not comfortable with who you are, you may just remain timid and keep to yourself, even though there is an opportunity for you to widen your social circle through making small talk. Thus, the key to being comfortable enough to make small talk is to try and feel comfortable when you are with other people. Remember that you are not the only one who feels awkward deep inside – the person you are talking with most probably feels that way too! So to save yourself the trouble, you should muster enough self-confidence to make small talk and be a social success.

Remember that practice makes perfect.

Don't you just envy the ability of other people to make strangers feel perfectly at ease by engaging them in small talk and a short, friendly conversation? If you do not have the natural inkling to engage in small talk, practice.

If you have never called your landlady by her first name, start getting to know her more by casually chatting with her. If you happen to see tourists or new faces in town, try welcoming them in the neighborhood by engaging them in small talk. You need to start somewhere if you would like to develop those 'rusty' conversational skills.

Broaden your knowledge of a wide range of topics.

The weather is probably one of the most worn-out topics of conversation between strangers. To move on from this topic to something more, try broadening your knowledge of a wide range of topics by reading everything from newspapers to magazines to the latest New York Times bestseller. Then, watch television and get updates on the news, sports, current events, even politics. It is easier to kick off the small talk if you know many topics that will interest others.

Ask questions and listen.

One of the misconceptions that many people have when making small talk is that they feel that they have to do all the talking. Remember that a good conversation is a two-way street. You also need to be polite enough to express interest in what the other person has to say. You can even 'listen' for clues on what seems to be interesting to that person, and the conversation should kick-off to something more interesting from there.

Asking questions is also an important part of making small talk. By asking questions that may or may not relate to what has already been said, you give them an excuse to continue chatting with you, essentially breaking the ice and getting rid of any awkwardness.

By following these small talk tips, you will benefit in such a way that you will survive any potentially awkward social situation. Engaging others in small talk is also a polite gesture, and not only that, but it also helps boost your confidence and widens your social circle. By giving the 'go' signal to others that you are easy to talk with, they will feel comfortable enough to respond to your attempt at making small talk.

3 Keys to Better Small Talk Conversations

Do you want to know how to overcome the challenge of not having anything interesting to say? Some people are afraid of striking up a casual conversation with a total stranger or with people they would not normally talk with because they fear not having anything interesting to say.

Fear of rejection is also another obstacle to making small talk. Remember that small talk in a conversation merely serves as a point to warm up to each other and get to know each other - the point is that you can get things going by talking about mundane and trivial topics, which is more acceptable than suffering from an even more awkward silence. **Take a look at some of these tips for small talk conversation:**

Try to make the other person feel comfortable.

No matter how successful they are at work or how confident they are with themselves, some people seem to shrink at the thought of having to make small talk. They find the entire process uncomfortable, awkward, even pointless. However, if you stick to this way of thinking, you will have a pretty small world if you refuse to let others in.

The key is to think that the other person may feel even more uncomfortable than you do - so if you will not make the first move to start the small talk, who will? So instead, try to make the other person feel comfortable by starting off with a casual comment or question, or even greeting them with a simple 'Hi' or 'Hello.'

Find a general point of interest and start off from there.

Once you have made the first move and uttered the first word when making small talk - there is no turning back. You need to keep things going - at least for the next couple of minutes or so - before you can gracefully say your good-byes and make a polite exit. So what do you talk about in the meantime? Think about what you would like to share with a new friend, which you can ask the other person about. Work, family, where they live, and their hobbies or interests are some general discussion points.

To keep the ball rolling, you can use follow-up questions to show that you are interested in what they have to say. Restaurants, movies, music, news, the weather, traffic, favorite tourist, or vacation spots are other things that you can use as small talk topics of conversation. Once you find common points of interest, things will take off from there.

Remember that small talk equates to casual and brief conversations.

Small talk can turn out to be a pleasant and gratifying experience. What you need to remember is that your conversation should be brief and casual without turning it unnecessarily into a long, drawn-out, and boring conversation that could even take an awkward turn. Instead, listen intently, ask questions and go out of your way to make the other person feel as comfortable as possible.

If it is the other way around and you are the one who is being asked to join in casual chitchat, do not turn out to let yourself dominate the conversation. Instead, think of small talk conversation as a juggling act, where the ball does not need to stay too long in one hand, and everybody should get to participate. Stop worrying about how big of a fool you may appear to be instead of focusing on what the other person has to say.

You may even find out later that you have the 'talent' of getting people to open up to you by engaging them in small talk. So in no time at all, your insecurities about being rejected should you make the first move in a casual scenario will be all for nothing – because you may have the knack for making small talk conversation!

How to Make Small Talk - You Can Do it!

Social communication is a very important part of our social skills. From time to time, people find themselves in situations where they have to start or engage in informal discussions. This is often known as small talk. Your ability to interact with others in a free and easy way, with the other party feeling comfortable as well, can be an invaluable asset to you.

While some people seem to know how to make small talk instinctively, others lack the required social skills to cope with small talk effectively or even at all. Moreover, since small talk does not focus on any particular topic, many people find it difficult to manage smoothly without stalling like a deer in headlights or just retreating somewhere else, out of sight.

Situations That Call for Small Talk

There are certain situations where people will be involved in informal conversations. However, social settings and events account for the bulk of instances when you will be required to interact with others largely by social behavior expectations.

Mostly, these will be with people you know little or nothing about other than maybe their name.

For instance, conversation starters will come in handy at a party, in an office environment, in striking up a conversation with a member of the opposite sex, and when you meet strangers, be it at a bus stop or while you are on a flight. In such cases, how well the conversation goes will be largely determined by how one or other of you breaks the ice.

Advantages of chit-chats

The advantages of these conversations and discussions cannot be emphasized enough. A chat of this nature may lead to many benefits in the future.

Small talk is one of the best ways that you can meet new people.

In addition, through small talk, you can develop a new interest, friendships can blossom, networking opportunities can be created, and everyone involved can be inspired, making them better people in the future.

With the benefits that these seemingly unimportant (even trivial) chit-chats carry, people need to learn the social skills necessary for such informal communication.

Tips on how to make small talk

Using the following tips will result in friendly chats with strangers being fun, informative, and memorable rather than scary events that are best avoided at all costs.

- **Avoid questions that require yes or no answers** – open-ended questions have the advantage of allowing the conversation to flow. Questions that require yes or no answers may end the talk after the answer, leaving an embarrassed silence.

- **Build the conversation** – you can ask about the activities or interests that your conversation partner mentions in chatting. This will help you build the conversation.
- **Keep abreast of current affairs** – small talk is not based on anyone's particular topic. Therefore, keeping up to date on various issues will help you keep your conversations interesting and informative. Just be sure to avoid controversial issues such as religion or politics.
- **Listen to the other person** – this is an important communication skill regardless of whether it's small talk or a more in-depth conversation. Paying attention will help you be a good listener, which is an equally important skill.
- **Keep your body language in check** – Simple things like not crossing your arms, keeping a good gap between you and the other person, and smiling all help.
- **Practice** – being shy does not improve your social skills! However, practice will help make you a better person to converse with.

All in all, the next time you are at the dentist's office, in a bank queue, at a party or a wedding, or any other public event where you meet new people, striking up a conversation should not be difficult.

With the tips I've just given you on making small talk, you should begin to find things gradually getting easier.

Conclusion

You might be wondering if there are ways for you to learn how to make small talk. It is important to learn how to make small talk because you never know when you might need to show that you know how - like when you have to attend a community function that requires striking up a pleasant conversation with a group of total strangers. You will need to know how to make small talk then.

Many people are quite comfortable speaking with strangers; if they don't have a purpose for the conversation they understand, they can struggle to make small talk. All social and work situations begin with small talk, where you make an effort to engage with people. If you are going to connect with people around you, you need to know how to make small talk.

The problem is that knowing how to make small talk can be very difficult for some people. They can even be nervous making everyday conversations with people, and often the reason behind this nervousness is a lack of knowledge of what to talk about. But you can acquire this skill of making small talk.

Small talk works wonders. Done properly, it will positively display your best qualities. It will build trust, respect, and comfort. You will get valuable information about the other person. And you will bond with them. And since it is just small talk, no one is very invested in the conversation. If you don't like the topic at hand, don't pretend to like it. Just talk about something else.

Try to overcome any feelings of shyness or lack of self-confidence by participating in more opportunities to do small talk. There's no getting around it - you learn how to make small talk by doing small talk whenever and wherever you can.

Always remember that small talk is a tool that can open doors that you would never expect. Practice it as often as possible and develop this skill to see the benefits it can provide.

Finally, if you found this book useful in any way, a review is always appreciated!

Further Reading:

EFFECTIVE LISTENING SKILLS - Learn Effective Communication, The Importance of Listening, Improve Your People Skills and Communication in Relationships

IMPROVE YOUR CONVERSATIONS - How to Talk to Anyone, Improve Your People Skills and Communicate Effectively

www.ingramcontent.com/pod-product-compliance
Lightning Source LLC
Chambersburg PA
CBHW061513250726

48657CB00005B/1841